Des MacHale

Seen & heard

In Ireland

Des MacHale

Seen & heard

In Ireland

GEMS OF IRISH WIT AND CONVERSATION

POOLBEG

Published 2008
by Poolbeg Press Ltd
123 Grange Hill, Baldoyle
Dublin 13, Ireland
E-mail: poolbeg@poolbeg.com

Typesetting, layout, design © Poolbeg Press Ltd.

13579108642

A catalogue record for this book is available from the British Library.

ISBN 978-1-84223-361-0

Typeset by Patricia Hope, Skerries , Co. Dublin

Printed by
CPI Cox & Wyman, Reading, RG1 8EX, UK

www.poolbeg.com

About the Author

Des MacHale was born in Castlebar, County Mayo some time ago. He lives with his wife Anne and their five children in Blackrock, Cork and teaches mathematics at UCC. He has written over sixty books which have been translated into many languages. His books include the Wit series of quotations, Lateral Thinking Puzzles (with Paul Sloane), two books on John Ford's movie The Quiet Man, a biography of George Boole, and many joke books, including Mayo Football Jokes, Kerryman, Corkman, Cavanman Jokes, as well as Malapropisms, Irish Bulls, Póg Mo Stone and The Jesus Jokebook. He regards Irish wit and conversation as the best in the world and this book is a tribute to the gems he has seen and heard in Ireland over the years.

Introduction

If you keep your eyes and ears open in Ireland you will see and hear lots of things – strange things, weird things, delightful things and, above all, funny things. Comedians find it hard to make a living in this country and most of them have to emigrate, because the competition is just too fierce from over five million unpaid natural comedians. Every pub, school, office, factory floor, golf club, and any other place you care to mention in Ireland has its quota of comedians who never go off duty. Add to this the unconscious comedians – people who are extremely funny without trying to be funny or sometimes even realising they are funny, and that doesn't leave a lot of us to make up the audience. In this book I have recorded the funniest things that I have ever seen or heard in Ireland – all of them of course "true", because even if you tried, you couldn't make them up.

Humour ⟩

Wit ⟩

Laughter ⟩

There was a big boxing match in Cork's City Hall and two clumsy locals were slugging it out in a preliminary bout before the main heavyweights on the programme. They didn't have a lot of skill and it was clinch after clinch after clinch. Finally, as the referee attempted to separate them for the umpteenth time, a voice from the back rang out:

"Switch out the lights, ref, they're in love."

Two auld wans were eating in McDonald's in Mullingar and were clearly enjoying this novel experience.

"Well, what do you think of McDonald's?" one asked the other.

"Very nice," she replied, "He's done very well for himself since he had that farm."

Two workmen in Galway were ordered to dig a hole in the road and were a bit worried about being hit by passing traffic. They decided to put up a notice to warn motorists in the area. It read:

RODE UP

Two women were sitting upstairs in a bus in Dublin having a chat on their way to town.

First woman: "I don't know what to get my cat to eat."

Second woman: "Have you tried Kit-e-kat?"

First woman: "No, he doesn't like chocolate."

A drunken man wandered into the ladies of a hotel in Athlone by mistake and was heading for a cubicle, unzipped and ready for action.

"Excuse me," squealed an elderly matron, "this is for ladies only."

"So is this madam, so is this."

The scene is a church in the west of Ireland during the Easter week ceremonies on Holy Saturday night. As the priest is leading the congregation in renewing their baptismal vows, a drunk wanders into the church and sits in one of the seats at the back.

"Do you renounce Satan, and all his works and pomps, and all his empty promises?" the priest asks the congregation.

"We do," shouts the drunk, "**** him."

A fellow went into a chemist's shop in Castlebar and said to the chemist:

"Could I have some Viagra Light please?"

"Viagra Light?" said the chemist. "I never heard of that. What do you want it for?"

"I need something," said the fellow, "to stop me pissing on my shoes."

Small ads in the Evening Herald:

WIDOWS WASHED. TALLAGHT AREA.

and this one:

STRADIVARIUS FOR SALE. FINGLAS AREA.
BARGAIN, ALMOST NEW.

Two women in a café in Douglas in Cork were having morning coffee.

"And how are the grandchildren?" asks one, "What ages are they now?"

"Well," said the other, "the engineer is six and the doctor is four."

The final of a big quiz competition was in progress in Thurles.

Quizmaster: "What was the name of the first woman who ever lived?"

Contestant: "I don't know. Would you give me a clue?"

Quizmaster: "I shouldn't really, but alright – she had something to do with an apple."

Contestant: "Granny Smith!"

A woman boarded a bus with her son in Belfast and said to the driver, "One and a half please."

Driver: "That lad looks over fourteen to me."

Women: "How could he be over fourteen and me married only ten years?"

Driver: "Look, missus, I'm driving a bus, not hearing confessions."

It was the World Cup finals in Japan and an Irish fan had run out of money. Desperate to get in to see the match in which Ireland were playing, he nipped in and said to the fellow at the turnstile:

"Would 'oo accept a co-op butter woucher?"

Heard in a travel agent's office in Sligo:

Travel Agent: "Your flight leaves New York at 8.20 a.m. and arrives in Seattle at 5.30 p.m. with one stop en route."

Passenger: "What state is en route in?"

It was a party political meeting in Wexford many years ago, and the Minister of Agriculture was in full flight praising government policy.

Heckler: "Call yourself Minister for Agriculture! I bet you don't even know how many toes there are on a pig's foot."

Minister: "Why don't you take off your boot and start counting?"

Notice seen on a grocery shop in Portumna:

THIS STORE IS CLOSED FOR YOUR CONVENIENCE

A Dublin bus driver was fed up with people continually ringing the bell for the bus to stop.

"What the hell do yez think I'm drivin'? A bleedin' ice cream van, is it?"

Two fellows were on a bus in Waterford and one says to the other, "Are you reading that newspaper you're sitting on, Mick?"

"I am, Paddy," said Mick. So he stands up, turns over a page of the newspaper and sits down on it again.

A young fellow wanders into a Killarney drapery shop and asks if he can buy a cap.

"Certainly, sir," says the shop assistant. "What sort of cap?"

"One like my father wears, with a peak at the back."

A truck is making its way up Cork's Patrick Street. As the driver is stopped at the lights before Patrick's Bridge, his gormless and long-faced assistant sticks his head out the window to check the traffic.

"Pull your head in quick," shouts the driver, "or people will think I'm driving a bloody horsebox."

A fellow was talking at the bar in a pub in Virginia, County Cavan:

"I don't know where all this fuss about smoking is coming from. I've been smoking for forty years and there's nothing wrong with my lung."

A young fellow walked into a Kilkenny bookshop and walked nervously towards the counter.

"I'd like to buy a play by Shakespeare," he said to the pretty young assistant.

"Certainly, sir," she smiled, "Which one?"

"William," said the young fellow.

Two auld wans talking in a pub in Donegal:

First auld wan: "How is your son gettin' on in the army?"

Second auld wan: "He's gettin' on terrific. Only two years in uniform and they've already made him a court marshal."

On a library building in the west:

THE LIBRARY IS CLOSED BECAUSE OF REOPENING TOMORROW.

IT WILL REMAIN CLOSED AFTER REOPENING BECAUSE OF ANNUAL HOLIDAYS

A woman was doing the Stations of the Cross in a Dundalk church, but had started at Station Fourteen, "Jesus is laid in the tomb", and was working her way back to Station One, "Jesus is condemned by Pilate".

The parish priest was keeping an eye on her, so he went up to her and said, "You're doing the Stations backwards."

"I'm glad you told me that, father," she said, "because He seemed to be getting better."

8

An American tourist was being driven around Dublin in a taxi.

Tourist: "Say, driver, I notice you have streets here named after some of your greatest patriots – O'Connell, Parnell and Tone – but how come you have no street here named after your greatest patriot of all, Eamon de Valera?"

Taxi driver: "Well, it's like this, sir; we had no street long enough or crooked enough."

A man standing in a Dublin bar was going on about his wife:

"My wife, is she fat or wha'? Every time she opens her mouth a light goes on."

There was a knock at a door in Naas and the man of the house went to investigate.

"Would you like to join the Jehovah's Witnesses, sir?"

"Look, I didn't even see the bloody accident," he retorted, and slammed the door.

Two women were standing at a bus stop on the northside of Cork City on a freezing cold December day.

First Woman: "I don't know what to get my young lad for Christmas."

Second Woman: "Why don't you get him a book?"

First Woman: "Don't be daft, girl, he have a book already."

Sign seen on a Connemara pub:

GOOD CLEAN ENTERTAINMENT IN THIS PUB
EVERY NIGHT EXCEPT TUESDAY

A British politician was speaking at a public meeting in Belfast and invited questions from the audience.

One man stood up and asked him bluntly, "Are you a Catholic or a Protestant?"

"I'm afraid I'm an atheist," he replied.

But the man persisted, "Is it the Catholic God or the Protestant God you don't believe in?"

A priest in Wicklow was going through the envelopes that had been dropped through his letterbox. One contained a mass offering which was marked:

FOR THE HOLEY SOLES

Seen in a death notice in Mullingar:

NO FLORAL TRIBUTES PLEASE AS THE DECEASED
WAS ALLERGIC TO FLOWERS

O'Flynn was the doorkeeper on a Cork City inn in the nineteenth century. One night somebody scrawled on the door:

WHAT A PITY HELL'S GATE ISN'T MANNED BY O'FLYNN,
THAT SURLY OLD DOG WOULD LET NOBODY IN

A Dubliner was on holiday in Tralee and his watch stopped so he asked a woman in the street what time it was. "I'm sorry," she told him, "I'm a stranger here myself."

Two young kids were heard talking in Ennis.

First kid: "What do you think of all this God business?"

Second kid: "I don't know — it could be just like Santa Claus or the tooth fairy."

First kid: "Maybe, but if there's no God, who the hell opens the doors in supermarkets?"

A fellow applied for a job on a building site in Longford. The foreman said to him:

"I can't give you a start today, but if you come back tomorrow I might have something for you. The position is that I have a fellow here today who hasn't turned up for work. If he doesn't come again tomorrow, I'll send him home and you can have his job."

A fellow went into an insurance agency in Athy and asked if he could insure his car against fire.

The agent filled in the forms and as he was handing them over he asked the fellow if he would like to insure his car against theft as well.

"Don't be daft," said the fellow, "sure who'd steal a burning car?"

Two oul wans were out for a Sunday afternoon spin in their old Beetle car. Suddenly it ground to a halt and they got out to examine the problem.

First oul wan: "I think we have a puncture."

Second oul wan: "At least it's only flat on the bottom."

Conversation between two pensioners on a Dublin bus, one of them reading the Herald out loud to the other:

"That was a terrible bus crash in Spain, wasn't it? Fifty tourists killed," said the first.

"You're right," said the second. "There's nothing worse than being killed on your holidays."

Notice seen near Navan:

THESE GROUNDS ARE PRIVATE. TRESPASSERS WILL BE PROSECUTED WITH THE FULL RIGOUR OF THE LAW
SIGNED: THE SISTERS OF MERCY

13

A fellow working in the post office in Carrick-on-Shannon had the job of sorting the holiday postcards. One card he picked up read:

HAVING A LOVELY TIME IN THE WEST OF IRELAND.
LOVE KAY AND TOMMY.

Under the name of the people for whom the card was intended was written:

HAVE FORGOTTEN YOUR ADDRESS

A card game was in full swing in a pub in Thurles when there was a sudden silence.

"Hold on a minute, lads," a voice rang out. "Someone is cheating. He's not playing the hand I dealt him."

In a bank in Galway, a blonde slid seductively up to the teller's counter and asked if she could cash a cheque.

"Certainly, madam," said the teller, "but first can you identify yourself?"

The blonde reached into her handbag, pulled out a little mirror and looked in it. Then she said confidently, "Yes, it's me all right, I'd recognise that face anywhere."

A woman in Mallow told her neighbour that her daughter had just run off with a married man who had lost both his legs.

Sign seen in a shop in Tipperary:

MEN'S TROUSERS €10
THEY WON'T LAST LONG AT THIS PRICE

Two auld wans were passing a shop window in Sligo when they saw a toupee of luxuriant hair for sale for €500.

"Isn't it amazing," said one to the other, "how they can make hair grow on that thing but not on your head?"

Near Tullamore, a fellow in a car drove through a red light and was stopped by a guard.

Guard: "Didn't you see that red light?"

Motorist: "I did, guard."

Guard: "Then why didn't you stop?"

Motorist: "Because I didn't see you, guard."

A bloke was standing at a bar in Ballina wearing a pair of immaculately white elbow-length gloves.

"What's up with you," asked the barman, "have you had the operation or what?"

"No," said the bloke, "I just promised the wife I'd never touch a drink again."

Notice seen in a window in Athlone:

EXCELLENT TYPISSED AVAILABLE

Notice seen in a beauty shop in Bantry:

EARS PIERCED WHILE YOU WAIT
PAY FOR TWO AND GET ONE DONE FREE

Heard in a courtroom in Galway:

Prosecuting Council: "And where were you in the interim?"

Defendant: "I never set foot in the place."

A Killarney jarvey was singing the praises of his native Kerry to a group of tourists.

"We have the best climate in the world here," he told them, "but the weather ruins it."

Sign in the window of a Navan optician's:

IF YOU CAN'T READ THIS SIGN, COME INSIDE
YOU MAY NEED GLASSES

A Cork plumber took a tour of America and was viewing the great Niagara Falls.

"What do you think of that?" the guide asked him.

"If I had my bag of tools with me, I could fix the leak that's causing that."

Small ad seen in a Fermanagh newspaper:

MAN AND WOMAN WANTED TO MILK TWO COWS,
BOTH PROTESTANT.

The local fire brigade in Listowel was called out one dark night to deal with what turned out to be a miserable little fire. As the locals gathered to watch the action, one of the firemen called out to his chief:

"Maybe we should let it burn up a bit so we can see what we're doing."

A middle-aged man was sitting at a bar in Macroom, lowering pints as if there was going to be a shortage.

"You look very depressed, Con," said the barman. "What's the matter with ye?"

"I've missed three maintenance payments," said Con, "and the wife is going to repossess me."

The final of the All-Ireland Hairy Bacon Eating Competition was being held in Kenmare and the two local lads in the final were trying to intimidate each other.

"You're nothing but a miserable vegetarian," sneered the first fellow.

"Will we cook it or what?" smiled the second fellow.

A fellow was drinking at a bar in Castlerea and the barman said to him:

"Your glass is empty. Do you want another one?"

"Sure what would I want two empty glasses for?" said the fellow.

Sign in a restaurant in Mullingar:

EAT AT OUR RESTAURANT AND YOU'LL NEVER
EAT ANYWHERE ELSE AGAIN

Two auld fellas were upstairs on a bus in Dublin.

First auld fella: "Do you think it's going to rain?"

Second auld fella: "How would I know? I'm not a geologist."

The scene is a bookshop in Athlone.

Customer: "I'd like to buy a copy of Mein Kampf."

Assistant: "Is that the author's name?"

Customer: "No, Mein Kampf is German for My Struggle. It's by Hitler."

Assistant: "Hitler who?"

Customer: "I don't believe this."

Assistant: "Look, I can't be expected to know the name of every author in the world. Anyway, it's time for my lunch break."

Extract from a CV received by the Bank of Ireland:

HOBBIES: DONATING BLOOD. HAVE GIVEN OVER 21 GALLONS IN MY LIFETIME.

The following notice was seen on the banks of the River Shannon:

WHEN THIS NOTICE IS UNDER WATER
CAUTION IS ADVISED IN CROSSING THE RIVER
AT THIS POINT

Two fellows were in the queue for their dole money in Tallaght.

"I hear your daughter is doing research at the University, Mick," said one.

"That's right, Trevor, she's hoping to find a cure for wheatgerm."

A milkman in Limerick used to collect notes left for him on the doorstep. Among his prize items were the following:

NO MILK TODAY. IF THIS NOTE BLOWS
AWAY PLEASE KNOCK.

and

TWO PINTS OF MILK TODAY. BY TODAY I MEAN
TOMORROW AS I WROTE THIS YESTERDAY.

A fellow in Kilkenny went to the doctor with an intestinal complaint. The doctor examined him thoroughly and prescribed a course of suppositories for him.

When he returned a few weeks later the doctor asked him if the treatment had worked.

"Not a bit of it," said the patient. "I ate about a dozen of them and for all the good they did me I might as well have stuck them up my arse."

A plainclothes detective from Dublin was on his holidays in Kerry and wandered down town late one night because he couldn't sleep. To his amazement, although it was 2 a.m., all the pubs were open and pretty well full.

21

There was a guard in uniform directing traffic outside one pub, so the detective said to him, "What time do the pubs close around here?"

"Usually by the end of October," said the guard.

Sign seen on a garage in Mallow:

THE MAN WHO LENDS TOOLS IS OUT

A group of Irish tourists were in Italy and were viewing the famous Leaning Tower of Pisa.

"We had a tower like that in Listowel once," said one of the tourists to the guide, "but some local genius of a builder straightened it."

Extract from a speech by the Lord Mayor:

"The streets of Dublin are perfectly safe; it's the people who make them unsafe."

Small ad in a Donegal newspaper:

FOR SALE, 200 TOILET ROLLS. HARDLY USED.
UNWANTED CHRISTMAS GIFT.

In a survey about the Irish language conducted in
Connemara, the results were as follows:
Can speak Irish: 81%
Can't speak Irish   12%
Don't know: 7%

Extract from a letter received by the Irish Revenue
Commissioners, your friendly Income Tax people:
"Dear Sir,
Thank you for sending me your brochure which I have
read with interest. However, I don't wish to join your
club at the moment."

A woman in Portlaoise was looking at a blank sheet of
paper and crying her eyes out. A friend asked her what
was the matter.

"It's a letter from my son," she said. "He can't write and he knows I can't read, but it's lovely to hear from him anyway."

Two auld wans on a bus in Tallaght.

First auld wan: "My daughter is an opera singer. She's got a part in Madame Butterfly."

Second auld wan: "What part is dat?"

First auld wan: "She's the caterpillar."

A priest was conducting a Christian doctrine class in a school on the north side of Cork city.

"Where was Jesus born?" he asked the class.

"Not around here anyway, father," said one little fellow. "He fell three times and never claimed a cent in compensation."

Fintona is a little village in County Fermanagh, world-famous for its state of the art creamery. At a junior football match an opposition supporter shouted out, "Come on, Fintona, the home of the hairy butter." A bloody riot ensued.

24

Two auld fellows talking in Wexford.

First auld fellow: "I see the Opera Festival is starting next week. What's the first gig they're putting on?"

Second auld fellow: "I think it's the Marriage of Fig Roll."

Two fellows from Balbriggan were talking in a pub.

"I'm giving up the cigarettes," said the first, "and I'm using the nicotine patches."

"I hear they're very good," said the second, "but they're fierce hard to light."

Sign seen above the sink in a hotel swimming pool in Meath:

IF YOU ARE USING THE SINK FOR SHAVING,
PLEASE MAKE SURE YOU CLEAN THE
BOWEL AFTERWARDS

At one of the last concerts Frank Sinatra gave in Ireland the climax, of course, was his rendition of "My Way". A middle-aged woman sitting up near the front nudged her husband in the ribs and said, "He's singing it just like you do."

Two travellers were coming out of a provincial courthouse, having just got a divorce.

The woman was heard to say, "Oh the shame of it! What will people think? Us getting divorced after forty years of marriage."

"What are you going on about, girl?" answered the man, "Aren't we still first cousins?"

A fellow went into a pub in Dundalk and asked the barman if he could cash a cheque.

"Certainly," said the barman, so the fellow handed him the cheque.

The barman took a look at it and said, "Sorry, this cheque is crossed. I can't pay it over the counter."

"No worries," said the fellow, "I'll come round your side."

Notice seen in a Galway newspaper:

BECAUSE OF A LACK OF SPACE A NUMBER OF
BIRTHS AND DEATHS HAVE BEEN HELD OVER
UNTIL NEXT WEEK.

Two old Dubliners were reminiscing about their early days working in Guinness's Brewery.

"Do you remember the time your man Fogarty fell into Vat number 23," said one to the other, "and broke his pledge?"

O'Sullivan was in the final of a Cork pub quiz and the result was a tie. The quizmaster said the first person to shout out the correct answer to the next question would be the winner.

Quiz Master: "What is the international distress call?"

O'Sullivan: "Help!"

A very devout Englishman was in the Dingle Peninsula on his holidays and decided to go to mass locally. To his horror, the mass was completely in Irish and he didn't understand a single word. But he noticed that, during the half-hour sermon in Irish, one word was spoken in English throughout: "sobriety".

He noted in his diary afterwards: "Apparently no exact synonym in Irish."

Two auld wans in a Belfast bus.

First auld wan: "I'm thinkin' of shavin' my legs."

Second auld wan: "They say it's a great way of losin' weight."

A local member of Portmarnock Golf Club had never broken a hundred in his life but he loved golf so much that in his will he decreed that he should be cremated and his ashes scattered on the eighteenth green.

His loyal wife carried out his instructions to the letter and one Sunday morning was seen heading towards the eighteenth with an urn in her hands. She deposited the ashes on the green, but a sudden gust of wind blew them into a bunker.

An old fellow in Athlone was going on in a pub about how tough things were in his area when he was a kid.

"We had no radio or television," he told his listeners. "One night my father knocked a hole in the wall so we could see the wrestling in the house next door. Then we realised our neighbours had no television either."

A girl in Kilkenny went to a drug counselling service and told the doctor she was addicted to sniffing car brake fluid.

"That's very dangerous," said the doctor, "and it can kill you."

"I can stop any time I want," said the girl.

Notice in a hotel bedroom in Cahir:

IF YOU SMOKE IN BED PLEASE LEAVE US AN ADDRESS
TO WHICH WE CAN SEND THE ASHES

A nun in the Liberties in Dublin was teaching her class the parable of the Good Samaritan. When it came to the part where a priest passed the beaten-up and injured man by, she thought she had better explain that priests on their way to the Temple were not allowed to touch the injured or sick in case they became contaminated.

"Now class," she asked them, "who knows why the priest passed the man by?"

"I do," said little Jimmy. "It's because he saw the man was already robbed."

Two fellows in Galway were having a drink in a pub and they decided to meet again in the same pub at the same time on the same date ten years in the future.

Ten years went by and one fellow walked into the bar to find his friend, older-looking and much heavier, sitting on the very same barstool.

"I never thought the day we left I'd ever see you here again," he said to his friend.

"Who left?" asked the friend.

Two little boys were talking in Listowel.

"I don't know what age I am," said the first.

"Do women bother you?" asked the second.

"No, they don't," said the first.

"Then you're four," said the second.

Two Donegal men went on an expedition to the North Pole and when they returned home they were interviewed by newspapers, radio and television.

"Did you have an exciting journey?" a reporter asked them.

"Oh, it was fair enough," one of them replied, "though we had a bit of frost at Glenties."

Heard at a séance in Monaghan:

"Is there anyone there? Knock once for 'yes' and twice for 'no'."

Two election workers in North Tipperary were in a graveyard taking down names from the tombstones for use in the upcoming election.

As their list grew longer, they came across the tombstone of a Japanese gentleman who had died the previous year and as one of them began to write his name down on the list, the other said, "Jaysus, Mick, we can't put his name down, he's Japanese."

"Look," said Mick, "there will be no racial discrimination in our party."

A fellow was standing at a bar in Ballymena when the bloke beside him said, "You're not from these parts are you?"

"No," said the fellow, "but how did you know that?"

"You just left your glass down."

A middle-aged lady was in a doctor's surgery in Limerick complaining about chronic constipation.

"Have you done anything about it?" the doctor asked her.

"Yes, doctor," she replied, "I sit on the toilet for an hour in the morning and another hour at night."

"But do you take anything?" the doctor asked her.

"Yes doctor," she told him, "I always take The Irish Times."

Definitely a true one this — I heard it with my own two eyes. Mr Dick Haslam, local government official, was being introduced to a visiting English businessman:

"This is Mr Haslam, Limerick City Manager for over twenty years."

The businessman replied: "Sorry, I don't follow football."

Conversation heard at the Ryanair desk in Dublin airport:

"I have three suitcases here. I want the brown one to go to London Heathrow, the black one to Glasgow and the red one to Manchester."

"Oh, we couldn't do that, sir."

"Why not? You did it last week."

A middle-aged couple loved watching TV movies at their home in Roscommon. When pressed to name her favourites, the lady was heard to say, "I just love the Lone Ranger and Toronto."

Heard in the old ballroom in Pontoon:
   "Does the band do requests?"
   "Sure, what would you like us to play?"
   "Draughts."

Two auld wans talking in the snug of a pub in Sligo.

   First auld wan: "I see where Mary Muldoon has just cremated her fourth husband."

   Second auld wan: "Some of us can't get a man at all and others have husbands to burn."

At Shannon Airport a lady was boarding a flight for Spain. In a plastic bag she was carrying a small portable television set as hand luggage.

   "Why do you have that with you, madam?" an official asked her.

"I don't want to miss Fair City while I'm away," she told him.

"But Spanish television doesn't show Fair City," he told her.

"And that's why I'm taking my own set with me," she smiled back at him.

This fellow from Kinsale had a serious medical condition so he was in intensive care in a Cork hospital. After a few days he was taken out of intensive care and put back on the wards but he soon got bored and decided to discharge himself. When his family rang that afternoon to see how he was, the Pakistani doctor on duty said, "He's gone, he's gone."

His wife, thinking he was dead, sent the local undertaker into the hospital to collect the body, but when the undertaker arrived he was told the true situation and decided to head back to Kinsale to break the good news in person.

On his way home from Cork to Kinsale, who did the undertaker see hitching a lift on the side of the road but the patient, so he stopped the hearse and gave him a lift home in the front. The wife happened to be looking out the front window of her house when she saw her husband arrive sitting up in the front of the hearse. She at once fainted and had to be rushed to hospital – in the hearse.

Really, you couldn't make it up!

On an icy day in Clifden a local slipped on the pavement and slid twenty feet until he was stopped by a wall.

"Did you slip on the ice?" a helpful passerby asked him.

"No," he said, "I have a bar of chocolate in my pocket and I just wanted to break it!"

Notice on a Connemara pub:

OPEN SEVEN DAYS A WEEK
(EXCEPT TUESDAYS)

This fellow was playing in a football match in the Midlands and, as was his wont, used violently obscene language all during the match on teammates and opponents alike. After the match, he was mortified to see the man he had been marking with a clerical collar, realising that he was a priest.

"I'm really sorry, father," he said to him. "I'd never have used that language if I'd known you were a priest. I thought you were just a Christian Brother."

A woman in Ennis was rung by Pat Kenny during The Late Late Show.

"What are you doing at the moment?" he asked her.

"I'm talking to you on the phone," she told him.

Two Corkmen were sitting drinking in a pub spending their dole money.

"I'm fed up of this kind of life," said the first. "I'm thinking of emigrating to Australia. I'm told there are places there where there are diamonds lying all over the ground and all you have to do is bend down and pick them up."

"Bend down?" said the second Corkman.

A woman in Kildare was heard to say that her husband had had an autopsy, but not until after he was dead; otherwise, it might have saved his life.

Two ladies are having a drink in a pub in Dundalk when a fellow slides up to them and says, "Have you girls come out for the night and left Cinderella all on her own again?"

A fellow in Kinnegad wanted to cross a field in which there was a vicious bull, so he asked the farmer what precautions he should take.

"You could carry a torch," said the farmer.

"And will that keep me safe?" asked the fellow.

"It all depends," said the farmer, "on how fast you carry it."

This one is gospel. A fellow working in the sports department of RTÉ television received a letter from a woman in Donegal saying she loved snooker on TV but the matches went on too late into the night and she was losing sleep. She suggested how the frames could be shortened. "There is a guy with white gloves who keeps taking the balls that have been potted out of the pockets and putting them back on the table. If he could be stopped doing this, I'd get a night's sleep."

Heard at a football match in Cork:

A fellow walks up to a man in a white coat and says, "Two ice creams please."

"Look," says the man, "you'd better get your eyes tested. I'm a bloody umpire."

The editor of a newspaper in the west of Ireland received the following letter from a reader.

"Dear Sir,

Last week I lost my gold watch so I put an ad in the lost and found column of your newspaper. Yesterday I found the watch in the trousers pocket of my other suit. God bless your newspaper."

At an agricultural show in Wexford they had a children's competition to see which kid had the most unusual pet.

Third prize went to a little boy who had a monkey.

Second prize went to a little girl who had a snake.

But the first prize was carried off by a kid whose pet was a tin of salmon.

This fellow from Bantry didn't have a single hair on his head. But he had a tattoo on top which read:

I AM NOT BALD. THIS IS A SOLAR PANEL
FOR A SEX MACHINE.

This Wicklow fellow can't stand Daniel O'Donnell so as a joke his wife gives him two tickets for a Daniel O'Donnell concert for his birthday. In disgust, he goes out and nails the two tickets to a tree in the park. Next day, when he is passing by, he notices that the nails have been stolen.

Two women were heard talking in a pub in Killarney.

"I met a fellow in here the other night and he told me that if I went out with him, he'd give me the winner of this year's Grand National," said one.

"And did ya?" asked the other one.

"'Deed an' I didn't," said the first, "Sure I have only a very small back garden."

A teacher was teaching her class English on Dublin's northside.

"Now, boys and girls," she said to them, "we will do opposites. What is the opposite of buy?"

"Rob, miss," shouted the class in unison.

A marriage ceremony in a Carlow church was in full swing.

The bride was asked, "Do you take this man to be your lawful wedded husband?"

"I do," she replied.

The groom was asked, "Do you take this woman to be your lawful wedded wife?"

"He does," replied the bride.

The parish priest of a little West Cork village called on one of his parishioners who had recently had a baby. She invited him in and offered him tea and a homemade scone. As he rose to leave an hour later he said:

"Thank you for the tea, and the scone was delicious."

"Yes," she smiled, "They always taste better when you make them with your own milk."

A fellow in Kildare went into a barber's shop for a haircut and noticed that the barber's hands were very dirty so he complained to him about it.

"Look," said the barber, a bit annoyed, "Is it my fault that nobody has been in for a shampoo yet today?"

A prisoner in Mountjoy jail was banging on the door of his cell in the middle of the night and creating a terrible racket. Finally a warden went to his cell and asked him what was the matter with him.

"I just want to know the time," said the prisoner.

"It's 2008," smiled the warden.

Do you remember the old Lada jokes?

A fellow from Galway bought a Lada car but returned a few days later and complained there was no repair manual with it.

So the garage owner gave him a bus timetable.

Notice seen in a Cavan pub:

CREDIT GIVEN TO CUSTOMERS OVER NINETY
PROVIDED THEY ARE ACCOMPANIED BY
THEIR GRANDPARENTS

A fellow was giving evidence in a court case on Dublin's northside.

"Would you say you live in a rough area?" the prosecuting counsel asked.

"Look, your honour," he replied, "In my neighbourhood you could walk two miles without leaving the scene of the crime."

A little old lady from Athlone rang Eircom's complaint department.

"How can I help you, madam?" said a voice at the other end of the line.

"The cord on my phone is too long," she said. "Could you pull it back a bit on your side?"

This Garda in Longford stopped a Polish fellow who was driving his car at 140 kilometres per hour.

"Do you know you were well over the speed limit?" he asked him.

"Sorry, officer," said the Pole.

Taking out his notebook, the garda said: "I'm afraid I'll have to issue you with a summons. Name?"

"Stanislaw Michaelovich Zwlowskizy," smiled the Polish fellow.

"Well, I'll let you off with a caution this time, but don't do it again."

Seen & heard in

Irish Courts

The Irish courtroom is a place which at times beggars belief. Some of the things that have gone on there read like pure fiction, and yet they are all true for the simple reason that nobody could have had the imagination to make them up. In some of the following cases the names and locations have been changed to protect the guilty.

The scene is a Dundalk court where a man is charged with having his dog driving his car. A garda gave evidence that the dog was sitting on the man's knees steering the car with his paws while the man manipulated the clutch and brake with his feet.

"Look," said the judge, "I saw a horse talking on the television myself the other night. Case dismissed."

A fellow in southwest Munster (one cannot be more specific for legal reasons) was charged with having unlawful carnal knowledge of a goat and opted for trial by jury. The sergeant gave evidence that he had looked through the window of the defendant's house and seen him perform intercourse with the goat on the kitchen table.

"Then", he added, "when it was all over, he and the goat had a long passionate kiss."

At this, one member of the jury turned to another and said, "Right enough, a good goat will do that for you."

A man in a Wexford court was charged with a number of offences under the Road Traffic Act. The prosecution's case referred mainly to the condition of the man's car and the list of alleged offences included the following:

1. All five tyres, including the spare, were bald.

2. Many of the car's parts, including the doors and exhaust pipe, were held together or supported with heavy-duty twine.

3. The driver had no tax, insurance, or driving licence.

4. Instead of car seats, there were four kitchen chairs, again secured with heavy-duty twine.

5. The steering wheel was not attached to the vehicle, and at one stage the accused was alleged to

have held it out of the window and waved it to a passing friend.

6. The brakes were non-existent and the only way the driver could attempt to stop the vehicle was by trying to throw it into reverse gear.

When the garda giving evidence first heard the car approaching, he thought there had been an explosion in the vicinity. When questioned, the driver admitted that he had bought the car from a passing motorist for £30 but had hopes of selling it to a transport museum for £100.

A driver in a Cavan court was charged with driving a car while eating two ice cream cones, one in each hand.

No need to change any facts on this one because for many years in Sligo the following nameplate was displayed on the town's most famous legal firm:

ARGUE AND PHIBBS

(Not to be confused of course with the name of an American law firm, DEWEY CHEATHAM AND HOWE – absolutely authentic.)

Before a certain Irish barrister was raised to the bench he was known to all and sundry as Necessity – the reason given was that necessity knows no law.

The defendant in a court case in Mullingar was very nervous.

"Do you plead guilty or not guilty?" the judge asked him.

"Not guilty, your honour."

"Were you ever in court before?" continued the judge.

"No, your honour," replied the defendant, "I've never been caught stealing anything before."

The court erupted, and the judge shouted, "Order now please, order."

"I'll have a pint," said the defendant.

Notice seen in Cork Prison in the nineteenth century:

Somebody stole a bottle of whiskey from the governor's office last night. If we catch the prisoner who did it, he will be expelled from the prison.

Heavy irony is a very dangerous weapon to use on an Irish jury. A celebrated barrister in a burglary case in Galway in the 1920s addressed the twelve good men and true as follows:

"If you believe, gentlemen of the jury, that the accused was merely walking across the rooftop on an evening stroll and that he happened to have with him a bag containing several housebreaking instruments with no intention of dishonestly employing them, you will of course acquit him."

Listening intently to the great man, the jury returned a verdict of "not guilty".

A riot involving a number of travellers was being tried in a Limerick court.

A clever young defence lawyer decided that he had a witness on the run and pounced on what he felt was a gap in his evidence.

"So you admit," he said triumphantly, "that you did not actually see my client bite off the plaintiff's nose?"

"That is correct," said the witness, "I didn't actually see him bite it off, but I saw him spit it out."

A husband and wife in Tipperary were having the mother of all arguments.

"Yes, I admit I like spending money," she screamed at him, "but name one other extravagance."

Genuine notice seen on a Cork City street:

THIS IS A ONE WAY CUL-DE-SAC AT BOTH ENDS

This one comes from a school in Galway. A pupil went to his teacher and told her that one of his classmates had called him a bad word.

"What word?" asked the teacher.

"It's so bad, I couldn't say it."

"Well, spell it then."

He called me a ******* p-i-g."

A builder's labourer from Roscommon went to the doctor suffering from severe constipation.

"Undress," said the doctor, "and lie face downwards on the treatment table."

The fellow did so, whereupon the doctor took a baseball bat and hit him an unmerciful blow on the buttocks.

"Right," said the doctor, "you should be fine now, and don't wipe yourself with cement bags in future."

Overheard in a ballroom in Sligo:

He: "Can I have the last dance?"

She: "You're havin' it."

Two Gardaí chased a man in their squad car on the dual carriageway near Ennis until they finally forced him to stop.

"Did you not hear our siren?" they asked.

"I did," he told them.

"Then why didn't you stop?"

"My wife ran away with a policeman, and I was terrified you were bringing her back."

Two house painters were working on a job in Nenagh. The assistant was up the ladder painting away and the boss was on the ground.

Boss: "Have you a firm grip on the brush?"

Assistant: "I have."

Boss: "Well, hold on tight because I'm taking the ladder away."

A statistician was doing research on the population of each Irish county and found to his amazement that Cavan, despite its size, had the smallest number of people of any county. He pondered on the fact for many weeks and finally wrote in his report:

"It appears that Cavan men don't like to part with anything."

It was the Limerick Rugby Cup Final and the scores were level with just a few minutes to go. One team forced a scrum near the other's try line but the defence was solid. Then the attackers tried the oldest trick in the book. One of them said to the defending hooker:

"How is your sister, the prostitute?"

Naturally, the hooker, Mickser, ups and punches the offender in the jaw and gets sent off. Penalty under the posts and the match is over after the resulting kick.

In the dressing room afterwards, the captain says to Mickser, "Why did you do it, why did you do it?"

Mickser: "Did you hear what he called my sister?"

Captain: "But Mickser, you haven't got a sister."

The singer at a Wicklow concert was in a generous mood so he asked the audience if they had any requests.

"Sing the Wendy song for us," shouted a man near the back.

"What Wendy song?" asked the puzzled singer.

"You know," said the man, "'Wendy red red robin comes bob bob bobbin' along.'"

Notice in an auctioneer's in Galway:

THE HIGHEST BIDDER TO BE THE PURCHASER
UNLESS SOMEBODY BIDS MORE

Two old ham-actors found themselves stranded in Athlone with the possibility of an engagement in Limerick, but they had no money for the fare. In desperation, they hitched a lift on an old barge travelling down the Shannon.

51

At one of their ports of call an official shouted out, "State your cargo please."

"A load of cow manure and two actors," replied the captain of the barge in a loud voice.

"Still not getting top billing," sighed one of the actors to the other.

A guy was having a drink at the bar of a pub on the northside of Cork City when the fellow beside him said, "Would you like to buy a gold watch?"

"Let me see it first," said the guy.

"Ssh, the fellow beside you is still wearing it."

Notice seen in a Donegal hotel:

PLEASE DO NOT LOCK THIS DOOR,
AS WE HAVE LOST THE KEY

Two auld wans on a bus in Dublin.

First auld wan: "Me cousin Mick is thinking of having a lung transplant."

Second auld wan: "I wouldn't fancy that at all – coughing up someone else's phlegm."

52

This fellow from Belmullet was giving evidence in court.

"You say you are engaged to a girl in Ballina," the judge said to him.

"That's correct," said the fellow.

"But a few minutes ago you said you were engaged to a girl in Westport. How do you explain that?"

"I have a bicycle," said the fellow.

Heard at an international football match in Dublin:

"Steve Staunton is the biggest waste of money since Madonna's mother bought her a new pair of pyjamas."

The judge was passing sentence in a Mullingar court.

"Prisoner at the bar," he said, "do you have anything to say before I pass sentence?"

"**** all," said the prisoner under his breath.

"What did he say?" said the judge to the clerk of the court.

"He said **** all, m'lud," said the clerk.

"That's funny," said the judge, "I could have sworn I saw his lips move."

A Belfast publican picked up the phone and was told there was a bomb in his pub that would go off in five minutes.

"Last orders there, gents," he shouted.

Three fellows walked into a bar in Dingle and one of them went up to the counter and said to the barman, "Three pints of Guinness, please."

Then he turned to his friends and asked, "What are you lads having?"

Two old ladies from Youghal were watching water-skiing for the first time. As a lovely young lady whizzed by them on the water front, one said to the other: "I can't see her ever catching up with that boat."

A pickpocket was being tried at a Cavan court.

"I fine you €200," said the judge.

"I have only €100 to my name," said the man, "but if your honour would allow me to mingle with the crowd in the courthouse for just a few minutes . . ."

A man received the following letter from Eircom:

"Dear Sir,

We have attempted on several occasions to contact you by telephone to discuss the payment of your long

outstanding account for your telephone, which was
disconnected some time ago."

Two auld wans in a bus in Belfast.

First auld wan: "Isn't it terrible about all them
icebergs melting?"

Second auld wan: "It's the greenfly effect."

A fellow in a Dublin pub was complaining to the landlord
about the bad quality of the pint he had just consumed.

"What are you on about?" retorted the landlord.

"You only had a pint. I have over a hundred barrels
of the stuff out the back."

A little lad was with his mother in church in Tuam when
he felt unwell.

"Quick," said his mother, "outside you go."

A few minutes later he was back looking a lot better.

"Did you throw up?" she asked him.

"I did, mother," he replied. "There was a box which
said FOR THE SICK so I went all over that."

Notice on the counter of a grocery shop in Portlaoise:

MOTHERS ARE REQUESTED NOT TO LEAVE THEIR
CHILDREN SITTING ON THE BACON SLICER AS WE ARE
GETTING A LITTLE BEHIND WITH OUR ORDERS

This Pakistani fellow goes into a shop in Dublin and asks for some pepper.

"Certainly, sir," said the assistant, "What kind of pepper do you want? Black pepper, white pepper, cayenne pepper or what?"

"Toilet pepper," says the Pakistani.

A sad little story from Limerick. A little fellow came home from his first day at school bawling crying.

"What's the matter, love?" his mother asked him.

"The teacher told me to sit in the front desk for the present," he bawled. "But she never gave me the present."

A man working in the Customer Services Department of Irish Biscuits told me he once received the following letter:

56

"Dear Sir,

Sometimes when I buy a packet of your biscuits, I notice the top biscuit is all broken and crumbly. I suggest that in future you would consider not putting a top biscuit in each packet."

That certainly takes the biscuit!

As a special treat for their wedding anniversary, a man took his wife to see a Shamrock Rovers versus Shelbourne football match in Dublin. But she spent so long getting ready that by the time they reached the ground it was already half an hour into the match.

"What's the score?" the disgusted husband asked a man standing beside them.

"Nil all," he replied.

"See what I told you?" said the wife. "We haven't missed a thing."

A lady went into a shop in Mullingar and asked the man behind the counter if she could try on the dress in the window.

"Go ahead, lady," he told her, "business is so bad that anything is worth a try."

The scene is a Dublin courtroom. A German sailor is up on a charge of being drunk and disorderly but can't speak a word of English.

"I cannot understand what this man is saying," says the judge. "Is there anyone here who speaks German?"

"I can speak German," says a man in the gallery, so he is sworn in.

"Ask him what his name is," says the judge.

"Vot iss your name?" says the man.

This fellow in Sligo wanted his house painted so he called in a painter for an estimate.

"I'll do it for €3,000," said the painter.

"€3,000?" said the fellow, "Rembrandt wouldn't charge that much."

"Well," said the painter, "if he does it for any less, he'll have to cross a picket line first."

This guy from rural Kerry went into a big drapery shop in Tralee and saw a pair of pyjamas for the first time.

"What are those?" he asked the sales girl.

"They're pyjamas, sir, you wear them at night," she told him. "Would you like to buy a pair?"

"No," said the Kerryman, "sure I never go anywhere at night except to bed."

Two women talking over a fence in Athlone.

"How is the son's business goin'?"

"Not so good. It's bein' put into the hands of the retriever soon."

At a certain third level academic institution in the south of Ireland, one of the professors was seriously ill in hospital.

The Governing Body wished him to get well soon by thirteen votes to twelve, with ten abstentions.

Notice on a farm in the Midlands:

MANURE FOR SALE
€1 PER PRE-PACKED BAG
50c DO-IT-YOURSELF

This fellow from Belfast was in love with a very beautiful girl but it turned out she had lots and lots and lots of other boyfriends. So before they got married, he made her promise she would never even look at another man and she gave him her word.

Then one afternoon he came home from work early and found her in bed with a dwarf.

"I thought you promised there would be nobody else," he screamed at her.

She screamed back, "Can't you see I'm trying to cut down?"

Heard in a Tullamore bookshop:

"Have you got Mrs Gaskell's Cranford?"

"When did she order it?"

A farmer from Dingle in County Kerry bought a new mobile phone and the first place he took it with him was to the bog cutting turf. After a few minutes there, the phone rang.

"How the hell did they know I was here?" he said to himself.

This fellow from County Down was a transvestite and he liked to play a lot of golf. However, he received a letter from the club secretary saying that he was being suspended and would not have his membership renewed.

So he sued the club for gender and sexual discrimination and took the club to court. The club pleaded "not guilty" and said he was being suspended for consistently playing off the ladies' tees.

At a wedding ceremony in Thurles, the bride and groom were happily marching down the aisle. A little girl and her mother were standing watching them at the end of their seat when the little girl said suddenly, and very loudly:

"Mummy, is this where he sprinkles his pollen all over her?"

Two old-age pensioners were sitting in a waiting room in Ballinasloe and the conversation went something like this:

"Me son is gone to America – he's living in a place called Gorilla."

"Do you mean Buffalo?"

"Yes, I knew it was the name of some big animal."

A Corkman looking the worse for wear was up in court on a charge of being drunk and disorderly.

The judge, a kindly soul, as many of them are, decided to adopt a gentle tone with the accused man.

"Tell me, Con," he smiled, "are you married?"

"No, your honour," replied Con, "I got hit by a car."

Sign in a Waterford restaurant:

CUSTOMERS WHO FEEL OUR WAITRESSES
ARE BAD-MANNERED SHOULD SEE THE MANAGER

This fellow who owned a big sports shop in Dublin was very socially aware and charitable so he hired a young traveller lad to work in his shop and gave him on-the-job training.

"Watch me now," he said as a woman came into the shop.

"Good morning, madam," he said, "how can I help you?"

"I'd like a tennis racquet," she replied.

"Certainly madam, for club or competition?"

"Just for club," she said.

"Well we have quite a selection, from €50 right up to €300."

"I'll have that one there for €150," she said, made her purchase and walked out of the shop smiling.

"Now you have a go," said the owner to the traveller lad as a man walked into the shop.

"I'd like a baseball bat," said the man.

"Certainly," said the traveller, "is it for a wedding or a funeral?"

A woman in Ballina was showing off her two new grandchildren, who were twins.

"Are they identical?" a neighbour asked her.

"Well, the boy is," she replied, "but the girl is not."

Two auld wans talking in a bus in Cork.

First auld wan: "Me son Frank is coming home from prison at the weekend."

Second auld wan: "But I thought he still had a year of his sentence to serve?"

First auld wan: "He's gettin' time off for good behaviour."

Second auld wan: "It must be a great consolation to you to have such a good son."

A little lad from inner-city Dublin was staying with relatives on a farm for the first time. One day he saw a cow sitting in a field chewing the cud contentedly.

"It must cost a lot," he commented, "to keep those cows in chewing gum."

Two auld wans were talking in a bus in Sligo about having a holiday in America.

"They say the skies are always clear and blue there," said one.

"I suppose," said the other, "that's because they have so many skyscrapers."

Little boy: "Mam, can I go to the Zoo to see the monkeys?"

Mother: "Certainly not! Imagine going to the Zoo when your Aunt Bridget is due to arrive any minute."

A man was in a train to the west of Ireland which stopped in Athlone for just a couple of minutes, so he stayed in his carriage and called to a young lad on the platform.

"Quick, get me a sandwich from the shop. Here's €10 and get one for yourself too."

Two minutes later the lad was back, saying, "Here's your €5 change, sir. They had just one sandwich left" – as the train pulled out of the station.

This fellow was retiring after working at the crematorium in Glasnevin for thirty-five years. His fellow workers gave him a barbeque set.

Notice seen in a Tipperary newspaper:

NEW BLOOD ALWAYS WELCOME
AT THE FENCING CLUB

This Polish fellow living in Wicklow was having trouble with his eyes so he paid a visit to his local optician to have them checked out.

"Can you read out what's on that chart for me?" said the optician.

"Read it?" said the Polish fellow, "I know that guy."

Two countrymen meet on the street in Claremorris.

"Did you go home yet?" asks one.

"No, did you?" replies the other.

Two fellows meet on the street in Clonmel.

"Jimmy," says one, "I heard you were dead."

"No," Jimmy replies, "as you can see, I am very much alive."

"Well, the fellow who told me you were dead is much more truthful than you are and I'd be more inclined to believe him."

An old woman in Derry was chatting about life and death with a friend.

"I'd like to live for a hundred years and a week," she told the friend.

"Why the extra week?" asked the friend.

"Well, I wouldn't like to die suddenly or anything like that," she replied.

An elderly American lady had a great time being shown round Killarney by a very enthusiastic jarvey and at the end of the day wanted to reward him.

"But I see a notice on your sidecar," she told him, "that tipping is forbidden."

"God help your sense, ma'am." he said to her. "So was eating apples in the Garden of Eden."

Mickey Martin lived in a makeshift hut on the outskirts of Castlebar. One evening he met the local parish priest out for a walk just as the Angelus bell began to ring. Mickey blessed himself, mumbled a few prayers and finished in record time. About three minutes later the parish priest finished and made the sign of the cross, saying, "You said the Angelus very quickly, Michael."

"Practice, father, practice."

Old Mrs Murphy is at the doctor's in Trim.

"And how is your insomnia, Mrs Murphy?" asked the doctor.

"Completely cured, doctor," smiles Mrs Murphy, "and it's a great relief to me. I lie awake half the night thinking how I used to suffer from it."

Little Jimmy from the Liberties in Dublin was heading off for the ice-cream shop with the euro coin his auntie had given him.

"Now, Jimmy," said his mother, "wouldn't it be kinder to donate that euro to the missions?"

"I thought about that," said Jimmy, "but I think I'll buy an ice-cream and let the ice-cream man give the euro to the missions."

In the old days in Connemara, a man called Pat O'Flaherty was up before the court charged with selling illegal whiskey or poitín. The prosecution built a water-tight case and it was odds-on that the jury would convict the man for the umpteenth time. But the defence lawyer had a brilliant idea.

"Members of the jury," he addressed them, "take one look at my unfortunate client, Pat O'Flaherty, with his red nose and unkempt dress. If he had a bottle of poitín, do you honestly think he would sell it?"

The jury immediately returned a verdict of "not guilty".

A fellow from Kilkee spent years in America as a builder and was boasting to his kids about the height of some of the buildings he had worked on.

"One of them was so tall," he told his amazed audience, "we had to lie on our stomachs to let the moon pass every night."

A woman knocked at the window of the ticket office in Athlone railway station and inquired of the clerk what the time of the next train to Galway was.

"It is half past three, madam," he said to her, "and that's the fourth time in the last ten minutes I have given you that information. Do you suffer from a bad memory or something?"

"No," smiled the woman clutching her little boy's hand, "it's my son Johnny here. He likes to see you come to the window. It reminds him of being at the Zoo."

"Now children," said a teacher to her kindergarten class in Ballinrobe, "no more questions please. Remember, curiosity killed the cat."

"What did the cat want to know, Miss?" asked a little girl.

A soldier at Cork Barracks was charged with climbing in over the barracks' wall at three a.m.

"Why didn't you enter by the main gate?" the commanding officer asked him.

"I was afraid of waking the sentry, sir," the soldier replied.

Sign seen in Ballyshannon:

LOW ESTEEM SUPPORT GROUP MEETS HERE EVERY SATURDAY AT 3PM.
PLEASE ENTER BY THE SIDE DOOR

A loan company in Dublin sent out the following polite letter to a client:

"Dear Sir,

We are surprised not to have received any repayment on your loan this month."

He replied:

"No need to be surprised – I haven't sent any repayment."

This fellow in Navan went to his local bank manager looking for a loan.

"Look," said the bank manager, "there's a little test I give to all my customers. I have a glass eye and if you can guess which one it is, you get the loan. Otherwise not."

"It's the left one," said the customer.

"Correct," said the bank manager, "how did you guess? Most people guess the other one."

The customer replied, "It had more warmth and humanity than the right one."

Two pensioners talking in a pub in Gort.

"How's the youngest son?" one asks.

"Oh, he's gone abroad to Israel."

"What's he doing there?"

"He's working on a kebab."

This fellow in Cork was unfortunate enough to have his house go on fire so he called the fire brigade on his phone.

"What action are you taking?" a fireman asked him on the line.

"I'm throwing water on the fire," he replied.

"Well, there's no point in us coming over – that's all we do."

71

Notice on a Drogheda dry cleaners:

DON'T DAMAGE YOUR FINE CLOTHES WITH A
WASHING MACHINE — LET US DO IT BY HAND

A huge Ryanair advertising hoarding read:

BREAKFAST IN DUBLIN — LUNCH IN NEW YORK

Underneath a wag had scribbled:

LUGGAGE IN HONG KONG

When the moon landing took place, RTÉ Television showed the action live. Their space correspondent lived in Naas so at one stage they went over to him to comment on the historic event. However, the link failed and RTÉ made the never-to-be-forgotten announcement: "We are having some problems getting through to Naas, so we now return you to the surface of the moon."

This fellow from Cavan was travelling by train from Dublin to Cork. He handed in his money for a ticket at Dublin.

"Thank you," said the ticket clerk. "Change at Limerick junction."

"I'll have my change now, if you don't mind," said the true son of Cavan.

An old fellow from the Liberties in Dublin was in hospital for the first time. On his first morning in the ward, a nurse asked him if he would like a bedpan.

"Do I have to cook my own breakfast here an' all?" he queried.

An American tourist was travelling in west Cork and having some difficulty finding his way when he spotted a farmer in a field.

"Sorry, Paddy," he said to him, "which is the road to Macroom?"

"How did you know my name was Paddy?" asked the farmer.

"I just guessed," said the American.

"Well, you can guess the road to Macroom too," smiled the farmer.

A young fellow joined a local radio station in Dublin and, just to test him out, the first assignment he was given was to interview a group of builders who were sitting on joists hundreds of feet above the ground. The reporter, who had an intense fear of heights, crawled nervously towards a builder who was sitting eating his sandwiches at the end of a long beam stretching up into the heavens. He put the microphone to the man's face and asked him, "Why did you take a job like this?"

The fellow answered, "I used to drive a school bus, but I lost my nerve."

An Irish judge was heard to remark: "We have the best legal system in the world. Every night we lock up the jury and let the defendant go home."

This fellow in Kinnegad hired a cowboy builder to build a house for him, but just before he moved in, the entire house collapsed.

It seems the builder removed the scaffolding before he put up the wallpaper.

"Granddad," said a little girl to her grandfather in Newry, "were you in the Ark with Noah?"

"No, love," he smiled at her, "I was not."

"Then how come you weren't drowned?"

Two women in a Limerick hotel bar.

"You'll have to excuse me for a minute now, Molly," said one, "I have to go and spend a penny."

"How are you going to do that, love?" said her companion. "There's no such thing as a penny now that they've changed the currency."

"Maybe I'll eurinate," she chuckled.

Pat and Mike, two lads from the south of Ireland, were walking through a forest in the Midlands when they saw a notice, which said:

TREE FELLERS WANTED

Pat turned to Mike and said, "It's a pity we didn't bring Sean with us or we could have landed those jobs."

A TD from Cork, who unfortunately will have to remain nameless, was travelling home by train from Dublin when he noticed a fellow eyeing him curiously across the carriage. He smiled back at him, because everyone has a vote, so the fellow came over to him and said:

"My wife is a great admirer of yours. I wonder if I could have your autograph for her?"

The TD was delighted to oblige and the fellow took the autograph saying, "That's terrific, the wife will be really delighted, because she's a great fan of yours." Then he said, in true Cork fashion, "Personally, I think you're a bit of a bollix myself."

At this stage the TD realised that the man very probably wasn't married.

Heard in Dáil Éireann:

Opposition TD: "The Minister hasn't got the intelligence of a donkey."

Ceann Comhairle: "Withdraw that remark immediately."

Opposition TD: "Certainly. The Minister has the intelligence of a donkey."

A young fellow from Mullinavat claimed that falling in love had affected his appetite. Before he met his girlfriend he used to eat ten slices of bread for his tea; now he eats only nine.

Sign in Navan pub:

> IF YOU SPIT ON THE FLOOR AT HOME PLEASE
> DO SO HERE ALSO.
> WE WANT YOU TO FEEL AS MUCH AT HOME
> AS POSSIBLE.

A teacher in a school in Clonmel was telling her pupils about the heroic feats of the ancient Romans.

"Some of these young men," she told them, "would swim across the River Tiber seven times every morning before breakfast."

Little Tommy, the class wit, raised his hand.

"What is it, Tommy?"

"Teacher, I was wondering why they didn't do it eight times and wind up on the side of the river where their clothes were."

Sign seen on a door in Dundalk:

WE CAN REPAIR ANYTHING
(PLEASE KNOCK VERY HARD ON THE DOOR
AS THE BELL IS BROKEN)

There was a house on fire on the northside of Cork city and three fire engines were rushed to the scene. However, the house was at the end of a lane which grew narrower and narrower so that eventually the three fire engines were trapped and couldn't move either backwards or forwards.

An old lady shouted at the firemen, "You guys better get your act together or that fire will be gone out."

A painter in Claremorris was working away painting a door at a rate of knots.

"Take it easy," said his mate, "remember, you're in the Trade Union."

"But I just want to finish the door before the paint runs out."

Two auld fellas in Wexford were watching an air display and marvelled at the pilots looping the loop, flying upside down and all the other acrobatics.

"I wouldn't like to be up there in one of them things," said one.

"And I wouldn't like to be up there without one of them things," countered the other.

On one unfortunate occasion at the Galway Hunt Meet, a bitch in heat was let loose with the hounds by mistake.

At one stage the master of the hunt inquired if anybody had seen the fox and he was told that he was lying fourth but gaining rapidly.

A middle-aged lady in Cahir paid over a hundred euro for a new hat and was wearing it going home when she was suddenly caught in a heavy shower. Instinctively, she pulled her skirt over her head to protect her new hat.

A passing gentleman said to her, "Madam, we can all see your bum."

"Look," she said to him, "that bum is over fifty years old, but I've just paid a hundred euro for this hat."

Dublin mother to her baby: "Assumpta, take your foot outa yer mouth. It's a fast day."

A little boy was an only child living in Killarney. He sent a letter to Santa saying: "Dear Santa, please send me a brother or sister."

He got a letter back from Santa which read: "Please send me your mother."

There was a time when Linfield football team from Northern Ireland came down to Dublin and beat local heroes Shamrock Rovers by one goal to nil.

Two Linfield supporters were returning home to the North with a few drinks under their belt. One turned to the other and said, "Man, there will be sore hearts in the Vatican tonight."

A fellow got a job as a builder's labourer in Waterford and the first day on the job he found his wheelbarrow filled to the brim with lead for roofing.

"Would you ever tie a couple of concrete blocks to my ankles?" he said to the foreman.

"What do you want me to do that for?" asked the puzzled foreman.

"To stop me from breaking into a gallop."

This lad from Listowel was a bit weak and spindly so he decided to take the famous muscle building course offered by Charles Atlas. After a few months he wrote a letter worded as follows:

"Dear Sir,

I have now finished the course. Please send on the muscles."

This fellow from Tullamore was up in court charged with stealing an overcoat.

The judge looked at him and said, "Weren't you up before me about five years ago charged with stealing an overcoat then too?"

"I was, your honour," said the fellow. "How long do you think an overcoat lasts?"

An American visiting Dublin sought out a house of pleasure and headed off to a bedroom with a beautiful girl.

A few minutes later, the girl burst from the room screaming hysterically, "I can't do that, I can't do that under any circumstances."

When the madam had calmed her down, she asked, "What does that pervert want you to do?"

"He wants me to accept payment in dollars."

A lad from Newport in the west of Ireland got a job in Dublin and was staying in digs.

On his first morning there at breakfast the landlady asked him if he would like beans on toast.

"Well, I normally have them on a plate," he replied respectfully, "but if you haven't got a plate handy, I suppose the toast will have to do."

An elderly lady in Edenderry met a young mother wheeling out her young daughter in a pram.

"What a lovely baby," she said to her. "What's her name?"

"Hazel," said the proud young mother.

"Hazel?" said the shocked lady. "There are a thousand saints in the calendar, and you call your child after a nut."

An Englishman on holiday in Connemara was delighted by the informality of the farmhouse he was staying in. In particular, he loved the way a little pig came in and nuzzled up to him every morning at breakfast.

"That's a very friendly little pig," he said to the farmer's wife.

"Not really," she smiled, "it's just that you're having your porridge out of his little bowl."

Brendan Behan used to say that one of the most beautiful sights to be seen in Dublin was the Corporation workmen breastfeeding their shovels.

There was consternation on a Galway building site.

"There's something missing," said the foreman, "every man on the site will have to be searched before he goes home."

"What's missing?" one of the workmen asked.

"A cement mixer," said the foreman.

Two families in Belfast were good friends despite the fact that one was Protestant and the other Catholic. One had a little boy and the other a little girl who liked to play together. One evening they both got so messy and dirty that one of their mothers put them both into a large tub and gave them a thorough bath.

Afterwards the little boy said, "I never knew there was such a big difference between Protestants and Catholics."

A census taker called at a house on Dublin's northside gathering information.

"Do you have a bath in the house?" he asked the woman who answered the door.

"We do, sir," she replied, "but thank God we've never had to use it."

Two Cork girls, Imelda and Attracta, were having coffee in a café.

Imelda: "I've just come back from this fantastic holiday – sun, sand and gorgeous hunks of fellows."

Attracta: "Where did you go, Imelda?"

Imelda: "I don't know, we flew."

Notice in a Cavan pub:

IN CASE OF FIRE PLEASE PAY FOR
YOUR DRINKS IMMEDIATELY

Jimmy from Carrick-on-Shannon was only seven but he had quite a sharp tongue in his head.

When his aunt gave him a present of a euro she asked, "What does a little gentleman say when he gets a euro?"

"I'm too much of a little gentleman to say," replied Jimmy.

An Englishman driving along the road between Ballinasloe and Athlone saw a farmer standing beside his gateposts each of which was adorned with a large concrete dog. Thinking to have a little fun with the locals he stopped and said:

"Say Paddy, how often do you feed those dogs?"

"Whenever they bark, sir," smiled the farmer.

In former centuries, the wit of the Irish ghillie or boatman was legendary. After a hard day's fishing, the Squire invited his ghillie around for a glass of whiskey, remarking that this particular blend was over fifty years old.

The ghillie looked at the miniscule glass he was given and remarked, "It's terrible small for its age, sir."

After he had gulped it down in one go, the Squire asked him if he liked the taste.

"I don't know, sir," he replied, "I forgot to taste it."

This fellow from down the country rang a ticket agency in Dublin and asked if he could have two tickets for Riverdance.

"Certainly, sir," said the girl at the other end of the line, "are there any particular type of seats you would like?"

"Two at the shallow end," said the fellow.

The Irish bagpipes are a fearsome instrument with a fearsome sound. As one commentator has remarked, we should be thankful they don't smell also.

An American visiting Cork stopped to listen to a bagpipe recital given by a street musician and as he slipped a few dollars into the cap he requested the piper if he would play his old mother's favourite, "The Banks of My Own Lovely Lee".

"But that's what I've just played," said the piper.

One of Ireland's greatest folk singers, Christy Moore, tells a lovely story against himself.

Christy would be the first to admit that he sweats a bit on stage, so much so that he often asks for a fan to be placed beside him to cut down on the perspiration. One night he was playing in a little hall down the country and asked for his usual fan, but the hall manager refused, saying, "A lot of the lads come in, not to hear your songs, but to watch you sweat."

A teacher in a school in Bantry was conducting a science lesson.

"Lightning is electricity," she told her class, "but with one important difference. What is it?"

"You don't have to pay for lightning, Miss," piped up one little girl.

A fellow took his girlfriend to a posh restaurant in Dublin and before the meal the girl started to say grace.

"You don't have to do that at all," said the fellow, "Shure I'm goin' to pay for this meal."

This guy goes into a chemist's shop in Bray and asks if he could buy some deodorant.

"Certainly, sir," said the girl behind the counter. "Would you like the rolling ball type?"

"No," says the guy sheepishly, "it's for under me arms."

Two auld wans again having a chat in the snug of a pub in Dublin.

"How's your son gettin' on?" asks one. "The one that went to London?"

"Fantastic," said the other one, "he's got a terrific job in a crematorium – burning Englishmen and getting paid for it."

There is a notice in a pub in Ennis which says:

ALL THE BEER YOU CAN DRINK FOR €20

A fellow swaggers into the pub and says to the barman, "I'll have €40 worth of that."

A lady went into a bookshop in Belfast and asked where the self-help section was. "If I told you that, madam," said the assistant, "it would defeat the whole object of the exercise."

A lady who had a stall in Dublin's Moore Street was filling some oranges into a bag when her friend from the next stall said, "Maisie, will you make yourself decent — one of your bare breasts is protruding through your shawl."

"Jesus, Mary and Joseph," said Maisie, "I've left the baby on the bus."

This fellow was up before the court in Clones charged with being drunk and disorderly for the umpteenth time.

"Look," said the judge, "you should be ashamed of yourself. You've been coming before me in this court for over twenty years now. What do you have to say for yourself?"

"Can I help it, your honour," twinkled the inebriated one, "if you never got promoted?"

It happened at UCC. A young lad up from the country met a professor on his first day and asked, "Which direction is the library in?"

"My good man," replied the professor, "you are now at university, and one thing we do not do here is end a sentence with a preposition. Now, would you like to try asking again?"

"Certainly," smiled the lad, "which direction is the library in, asshole?"

(AGAIN)

SOME CLASSIC IRISH COURT ROOM REPLIES:

"Prisoner at the bar, you have been found not guilty of robbery and are discharged."

"Thank you, your honour. Does that mean I can keep the money?"

"Are you the defendant?"

"No, your honour, I'm the fellow who stole the chickens."

"Prisoner at the bar, are you guilty or not guilty?"

"How do I know, your honour, until I've heard the evidence?"

"Do you plead guilty or not guilty?"

"What else have you got?"

"Did you sleep with this lady in Dublin?" the defendant was asked in an indecent assault case.

"No, I did not," he replied.

"Did you sleep with this lady in Cork?"

"No, I definitely did not."

"Did you sleep with this lady in Galway?"

"No way, absolutely not."

"Did you sleep with this lady in Athlone?"

"No comment," said the accused.

"Could the victim have been alive on January 13th?" an eminent forensic scientist was asked in court in a Dublin murder case.

"Absolutely not," he replied.

"How can you be so sure?" the defence lawyer continued.

"Because on that date," said the scientist, "his brain was in a jar in my laboratory."

In desperation, the defence lawyer continued, "Is there no way whatsoever that he could have been alive on that date?"

"No," said the scientist, "unless he was practising law somewhere."

"My client is an unfortunate Jekyll and Hyde character," said a solicitor in a Kilkenny court case, "and in the circumstances I think it is appropriate that bail should be granted."

"I am happy to grant bail to Dr Jekyll," said the judge, "but Mr Hyde is remanded in custody for seven days."

The judge in a Donegal court case said to the prisoner at the bar, "I am disappointed in you. Last time I let you off because you promised you would make every effort not to appear in court again."

"But I did, your honour," said the prisoner. "It took six gardaí to get me in here today."

One part of Limerick city was described in court as being so rough that all police leave was cancelled every time there was a Tupperware party.

A cheeky young prisoner in a Dublin court was chewing gum even as his case was being heard.

The judge called the court clerk and said to him quietly, "Tell that young man to desist from masticating."

The clerk whispered to the prisoner, "The judge says take your hands out of your pockets."

A farmer from Roscommon came home to his wife one night with his head covered in cow dung.

"What happened to you?" she screamed.

"Well," he said, "I took a short cut across the cow field and the wind blew my cap off. I must have tried ten caps before I found the right one."

An innocent young couple from Belmullet decided to spend their honeymoon in Dublin. When they arrived at their hotel bedroom, the new bride was dismayed to find that it had twin beds.

She burst into tears, sobbing, "I was hoping we would have a room to ourselves on our honeymoon."

In the middle of the night a couple in Kells hear a knock on their door, so the man sticks his head out the window and says, "What do you want?"

A fellow replies, "I need a push."

"Go away," says the man, "I've had a hard day's work and I need some sleep."

So the man goes back to bed and tells his wife what had happened.

"You should help him," says the wife, "just imagine how you would feel if you needed a push."

So, swearing to himself, the man gets up, goes out into the dark and shouts, "Where are you, I'll give you a push."

"Great," shouts the fellow, "I'm over here on the swing."

A flying saucer landed on the Garvaghy Road in the North of Ireland. Two little red men got out and one of the locals rushed up to them and said, "Are you Catholic or Protestant?"

"We are Martian," said one of the little red men.

"Well, you're not marchin' down here for a start."

A new mother in Dundalk went into a chemist's shop and asked for a packet of nappies.

"Certainly, madam," said the assistant, "that will be €8 and €1 for the tax."

"Don't bother with the tacks," said the woman, "I'll use safety pins."

Who says the spirit of entrepreneurship is dead in Ireland? During the Ulster Pride riots in Dublin a couple of years ago, two locals set up a stall on O'Connell Bridge with a notice:

STONES 50c; PORTIONS OF
CONCRETE BLOCKS €1

This Cavan man went to the doctor and was prescribed a bottle of pills. A few weeks later he was back complaining that he had got better before all the pills were used up.

Cork's Opera House is famous for its heckles and counterheckles. Try to heckle a Cork comedian and you will be hit with one of the following I have heard over the years:

Why don't you save your breath for blowing up your girlfriend when you get home?

Isn't it sad when cousins marry?

I know – that's how I felt too the night I had my first beer.

The last time I saw a head like yours, it was circumcised.

Haven't I seen you on television? He's called Interference.

One other crack like that and your wife and I are through.

What time is your mummy coming to collect you?

What are you going to do for a face when Quasimodo wants his arse back?

Look, I don't interrupt when you're working and tell you how to sweep streets.

Ad seen in a Northside newspaper:

FOR SALE. CAR.
AS SEEN ON CRIMELINE

Two fellows chatting in a pub in Wicklow.

First fellow: "Did you see the eclipse of the moon the other night?"

Second fellow: "No I didn't, but I listened to it on the radio."

Graffito seen in the Gents in Leinster House:

THIS IS THE ONLY PLACE WHERE WE KNOW WHAT
THE TAOISEACH IS REALLY DOING

This fellow from RTÉ decides to turn over a new leaf and begin practising his religion again. As a first step he decides to go to Confession after many years' absence. So he goes into the box and says, "Bless me father for I have sinned. I work at RTÉ."

The priest says, "Well done my son. It must have taken a lot of courage to confess that."

A woman went into the job centre and said, "Dick ack de neck boom an pillock tallin un will kad agum dhool amok."

The man in the job centre said, "Well, I have a vacancy for a platform announcer at Heuston Station, starting immediately."

The scene is the lost property office at Galway Railway Station. The customer has asked the attendant a question and the attendant replies, "No, it doesn't work like that. First you tell me what you have lost and I'll tell you what we have found."

A renowned Cork hurler qualified as an engineer and went to live in Tipperary where he practised his profession. Here he married and he and his wife had two little sons who followed the Tipperary hurling team avidly, going to matches wearing their county colours and waving the county flag.

All went well until the father took his two sons to the Munster final between Cork and Tipperary. In the final minute, Tipperary scored a goal, putting them a point ahead and heading for victory. As the two little lads cheered wildly, the father said to his sons, "Shut up, you little pair of bastards."

A kid in Junior Infants in a school in Trim was telling his teacher about a scary incident that had happened in his house at the weekend.

"My mummy was locked in the bedroom and couldn't get out," he told her.

"And why didn't your daddy get her out?" asked the teacher.

"He was locked in there with her," said the kid.

A teacher in Macroom was worried because Connie, one of his pupils, hadn't appeared in school for over a week. When he finally showed up he asked him why he had been absent.

"I was having a growth removed from my head," replied Connie.

"Goodness me, was that painful?"

"Not at all," smiled Connie, "it was only a haircut."

This Chinese tourist in Dublin is looking for the Botanic Gardens so he stops a local and asks him for directions.

"The Botanic Gardens," says the Dubliner, "I know that as well as me own house. Go up O'Connell Street, turn left. No that's not right. Go along the Finglas Road and turn left. No that's not right either. Tell me, do you know Slattery's Pub in Terenure?"

This woman is driving erratically on the Naas dual carriageway so she is stopped by a traffic cop.

"Could I see your licence please, madam?" he asks her.

"Look," she said to him, "last month my licence was taken away, and now you want to see it. I wish you people would make up your minds."

A fellow went into a post office in Headford and asked if he could buy a licence for his dog.

"Certainly, sir," said the assistant, "what name?"

"Spot," said the fellow.

Two Americans were in a pub in Kenmare, so they thought they would have a bit of fun at the expense of the locals.

"Hey, Mick," one of them said to the barman, "could you give me change for this twenty-four euro note?"

"Certainly," smiled the barman, "how do you want it – three eights or six fours?"

This Englishman was walking down the Falls Road in Belfast and not feeling very well so he stopped a local and asked him, "What's the quickest way to get to the nearest hospital?"

"Just walk into the nearest pub," said the local man, "and shout 'To Hell with the Pope'."

Two girls were enjoying a drink in a Limerick hotel when one excused herself and went to the Ladies. When she came back, her friend said to her, "Maisie, you've got a Tampax stuck in your ear."

"Mother of God," said Maisie, "where have I put my cigarette?"

Two middle-aged women were talking in a golf club in Dun Laoghaire.

"I don't know what to do about my husband," said one, "he smokes in bed."

"That's not the end of the world," said the other.

"But kippers?"

Sign seen in a shop in Derry:

UNATTENDED CHILDREN
WILL BE SOLD INTO SLAVERY

Iarnrod Éireann received the following letter of complaint from a passenger:

"The toilet on the Dublin-Galway train was a disgrace. It was like a shithouse in there."

Heard on Today FM radio station:

Compere: "What anniversary does bicentennial celebrate?"

Contestant: "Give me a clue please."

Compere: "Centennial is one hundred and bi means two."

Contestant: "I have it now – it's the hundred and second anniversary."

There is a new Irish boomerang for sale in the gift shops in Killarney. It doesn't come back – it just sings songs about how much it wants to come back.

This fellow living in Carlow goes to a psychiatrist and tells him he is worried because he is obsessed with collecting CDs and that he has over a hundred thousand of them in his flat.

"There's nothing wrong with that," says the psychiatrist, "I like a bit of music myself."

"But you don't understand, doc," says the fellow, "I don't collect them for the music, I collect them for the holes in the middle."

A new Irish proverb heard on RTÉ Radio:

"Knowledge is knowing that a tomato is a fruit. Wisdom is not putting a tomato in a fruit salad."

This fellow was living in Spiddal so he asked his wife what she would like for Christmas.

"Anything you like," she replied, "as long as it has diamonds in it."

So he bought her a pack of playing cards!

"Why don't you give up drinking, smoking and women?" a priest asked the most degenerate resident of Ballyshannon.

"It's too late," said your man.

"It's never too late," said the priest.

"Then there's no rush," said your man.

A fellow in a fish and chip shop is getting a bit impatient.

"Your fish won't be long, sir," said the girl.

"Then it better be wide," says the fellow.

A lady in Celbridge went into a shop and asked if she could buy some wool.

"How much wool does madam want?" asked the assistant.

"I'm not sure," she replied, "I'm knitting a coat for my dog for his birthday."

"Well, why don't you bring the dog in and we can measure him?" suggested the assistant.

"Oh, no, I couldn't do that," said the lady. "It's meant to be a surprise."

A Dubliner, a Kerryman and a Cavan man go into a strip club. They like the girl stripping so much that the Dubliner puts a €10 note on one of her butt cheeks. The

Kerryman, not to be outdone, puts a €20 note on her other butt cheek. The Cavan man takes out his credit card and withdraws €30 with a quick swipe.

A fellow runs out of a pub in Belfast with the sleeve of his jacket on fire. The police arrested him and charged him with having an armalite.

This couple from Tullamore had eighteen children so they went to their local priest for family planning advice.

"I'd recommend you use the rhythm method," he told them.

"Where are we going to find a céilí band at two o'clock in the morning?" said the husband.

A fellow in Listowel went to the doctor complaining that he always felt dizzy and lightheaded for an hour after he got up in the morning.

The doctor told him to get up an hour later.

A sadist living in Athlone has come up with a clever new scheme to solve the litter problem:

Give blind people pointed sticks.

A health inspector in Limerick complained to a café owner that there was a terrible smell on his premises and that maybe he should have his drains checked.

"Oh, it can't be the drains," said the owner, "because we have no drains."

This fellow in Sligo went into hospital to have a kidney removed. Three days after his operation there was kidney soup on the menu.

"Cripes," he said, "they waste nothing round here."

This lady in Moate had two dogs misbehaving outside her window at three o'clock one morning so she rang her vet for advice.

"Have a phone ring loudly near them," he said.

"And will that stop them?" she asked.

"Well it certainly stopped me."

Three kids in Dublin were boasting about how fast their fathers were.

"My father once beat Ronnie Delaney in a race," said the first.

"My father can fire an arrow," said the second, "and catch it before it reaches the target."

"My father," said the third, "is easily the fastest. He works for Dublin City Council. He doesn't finish work until five but he's always home by two o'clock."

The scene is Dublin Zoo where a woman is standing in front of the monkey enclosure but there are no monkeys to be seen.

"Where are all the monkeys?" she asks a keeper.

"They are all at the back of the monkey house, mating, madam," he told her.

"Do you think they would come out if I gave them some peanuts?"

"Would you, missus, would you?"

Two fellows from the south were travelling in the North of Ireland for the first time by train.

"Hey," one said to the other, "this is a pretty long tunnel – I wonder what it is called?"

"This is no tunnel," said the other, "this is Belfast."

Two women from Tralee were gossiping over the garden fence.

"So your daughter is married at last," said one. "Tell me, how is she getting on?"

"Oh, she's getting on fine," said the other, "lovely house in a lovely area, lots of money to spend. There's only one problem – she cannot stand her husband."

"Oh dear," agreed the neighbour, "there's always something, isn't there?"

A little corner shop in Cork is just about to close for the night when a drunk wanders in and says very aggressively, "Do ye have any broken biscuits?"

"I think we might sir," says the shop owner, seeking to prevent an incident.

"Well," said the drunk, wagging a finger, "you should handle them more carefully in the future." With that, he staggers out of the shop.

This fellow in Galway wants to write a letter so he goes into a shop and says to the girl behind the counter, "Do you keep stationery?"

She says to him, "I do until near the very end but then I go wild."

Sign seen in a pub in Carrick-on-Suir:

JUST BECAUSE YOUR DOCTOR SAYS
YOU NEED GLASSES
THERE'S NO NEED TO TAKE OURS

It happened at the rededication of Waterford Cathedral. All of the priests from miles around were taking part in a solemn procession to the altar. As one old priest was approaching the steps he slipped but managed to save himself from falling by clinging on to the ceremonial brass eagle that supported the bible.

Forgetting the microphone was live, he said to his companion, "If it wasn't for that ******* duck, I was a goner."

This Japanese fellow walks into a café in Dublin and the waitress says to him, "You for coffee?"

Very embarrassed, the fellow gets up and walks out.

A bus driver in Cork was daydreaming at the wheel a full ten seconds after the lights had gone green.

The conductor said loudly to him, "They won't get any greener, you know."

110

A woman was sitting on a bus going down the quays in Dublin. On her knee was a little lad of three or so and she was pointing out things for him to identify – bridges, cars and the like.

Seeing a seagull on the Liffey wall, she asked him, "What's that?"

"Donald Duck," he screamed in delight.

Two women on a bus in Dundalk and one of them is reading Teach Yourself Chinese.

"What are you reading that for, Mary?" one of them asks. "Are you going to China for a holiday?"

"No," says the other, "me son and his wife are adopting a Chinese baby and I want to be able to understand it when it starts to talk."

A Dublin woman at a bus stop with her eight kids of various ages. When a bus stops, she says to the driver, "Are we right for the zoo, mister?"

Bus driver: "You're perfect."

This American was sightseeing in Clifden and nearly fell over a cliff into the sea.

"Say," he said to the guide, "that's a pretty dangerous place. Why isn't there a sign warning people?"

"We had a sign there for years," said the guide, "but nobody ever fell over the cliff, so we took the sign away."

A builder's labourer in Monaghan needed to reach a floor on the second storey of a house. The longest ladder he had was too short so he found a wheelbarrow and used it to raise the bottom of the ladder!

Two girls heard talking on a bus in Limerick.
    "Then he put his hand up my skirt."
    "Not the red one with the blue flowers on it?"

Sign seen in Connemara:

LAST PETROL STATION UNTIL THE NEXT ONE

A little lad in Letterkenny was just home from his first day in school.

"Well, how did you get on?" his adoring mother asked him.

"Not a lot happened," said the little fellow, "except a woman didn't know how to spell 'cat' so I told her."

Notice in a Wexford department store:

CUSTOMERS ARE REMINDED THAT THEY
CAN TRAVEL IN THE LIFT
ONLY WHEN THE LIFT IS WORKING

It was the annual boat race between Trinity College Dublin (TCD) and University College Dublin (UCD) and this time UCD won by a mile.

However, the mother of the TCD stroke rushed up to her golden boy and threw her arms around him saying, "Tough luck, darling, it wasn't your fault you lost, but the fault of those second-raters you were in the boat with. You rowed better and faster than all of your crew."

Notice in a Tullamore pub:

WE OPEN AT 10.00 A.M. AND CLOSE PROMPTLY
AT 11.00 P.M. EVERY DAY. IF YOU HAVEN'T HAD
ENOUGH TO DRINK BY THAT TIME WE FEEL YOU
HAVEN'T REALLY BEEN TRYING

Two girls from the country in Dublin saw a fully kilted
Scotsman, over for the rugby international, for the first
time. One of the girls, more daring than the other, went
over to him and, fixing her gaze on his magnificent
sporran, asked him:

"Excuse me, what do you keep in your scrotum?"

A fellow from Skibbereen took part in the National
Poker Championship but came last. Every time he picked
up a spade he spat on his hand.

Ad seen in a Donegal newspaper:

HONEYMOON COTTAGE TO LET.
SLEEPS THREE.

A fellow living near the Cliffs of Moher invited a friend home for a meal and gave him a fine dinner of roast pork.

"That was a wonderful meal," said the friend afterwards, licking his lips.

"So it should have been," said his host. "That was none of your slaughtered meat. That pig died a natural death."

They have a colourful turn of phrase in Dublin pubs. If you listen carefully, you will hear gems like, "Brian Cowen is to politics what piles are to Ruby Walsh."

A woman runs into a café in Kildare and says to the waitress: "Give us a cup of tea, love, and a couple of suggestive biscuits."

Sign seen outside a church in Roscommon:

REPENT NOW! IF YOU HAVE ALREADY REPENTED
PLEASE DISREGARD THIS NOTICE

There was a fire in a lap-dancing club in Belfast recently. It took ten minutes to put the fire out and three hours to put the firemen out.

A Dublin woman is telling her neighbour that her son-in-law is in hospital for some tests.

"He's okay, though; he's on the VHI," she tells her.

The neighbour looks shocked. "God love him, how did he catch that?"

Sean: "I've been a foreman with Dublin Corporation for twenty-five years."

Andy: "That's a long time to be idle."

This woman from Skerries claimed she was the unluckiest person in the world. She paid €50 for a non-stick frying pan and couldn't get the label off no matter what she did.

Sign seen in an Indian restaurant in Dublin:

AFTER ONE VISIT WE GUARANTEE YOU WILL
BE A REGULAR CUSTOMER

This mummy's boy got a job as a tightrope walker with a circus in Waterford.

The manager asked him: "Can you work without a net?"

"No, my hair would be all over the place."

An enterprising shoeshine boy in Cork had a notice which read:

ONE SHOE SHINED ABSOLUTELY FREE!

The attendant at a public toilet in Dublin was giving evidence at a court case involving indecent behaviour on his premises.

"It was pretty disgusting what went on in there," he told the court. "In fact when anyone came in for a straightforward shit, it was like a breath of fresh air."

117

Two fellows the worse for wear met on a street in Enniscorthy.

First fellow: "Do you know the time?"

Second fellow: "I do."

First fellow: "Thank you very much."

A nun was conducting a religious class on Dublin's northside.

"Now boys," she said, "if any of you found a €50 note on the street, would you keep it?"

"No, sister," said the class in unison.

"Very good," she said, "what would you do with it?"

"Spend it, sister," said the class at once.

Two inebriates were staggering down O'Connell Street in Dublin late one night and decided to partake of a fried chicken repast.

As they staggered up to the door of a fast food outlet, the manageress came out and informed them "Sorry, we're closing for business."

The merry gentlemen proceeded to heap abuse on her. "She has a face like a bag of spanners," observed one of them wittily.

"No," said the other, "she looks as if she ran out of money half way through a sex-change operation."

Notice seen on an old folks' home in Longford:

OPEN DAY ON SUNDAY NEXT. DRESS FORMAL
TEETH WILL BE WORN

A fellow was walking down the main street in Boyle when he was stopped by another man.

"Jimmy," he said to him, "don't you remember me? We were in the same class in school together."

Jimmy took one look at him and said, "There were no fellows in my class with bald heads and moustaches."

A guy from Killorglin was a heavy smoker so his doctor advised him to go on the nicotine patches. He thought the way to use them was to plaster one over each eye so he wouldn't be able to find his packet of cigarettes.

A woman took her little boy on a visit to Dublin Zoo.

They stopped outside the stork's cage and the little boy stared at the bird intently for about five minutes. Then he burst into tears. "Mam," he wailed, "he doesn't even remember me."

A rich businessman in Athlone was fishing and fell into the river. His wife immediately rushed to the bank and withdrew all the money from their joint account.

Sign in a barber shop in Tralee:

> DURING RENOVATIONS CUSTOMERS
> WILL BE SHAVED IN THE REAR

"My wife has just eloped with my best friend," said a fellow to a barman in Templemore. "What was his name?" asked the barman.

"I don't know," smiled the fellow, "I never met him."

This guy was dancing with a girl in Galway. To make conversation, he said to her, "It's a nice floor for dancing, isn't it?"

She retorted, "Well, why don't you get off my feet and give it a try?"

A scruffy singer performing at an old folks' concert in Cork wasn't going down very well so in desperation he asked for requests. "Do you know 'The Barber of Seville'?" a voice asked from the audience.

"Yes, I do," he said eagerly.

"Well, go and get your hair cut then."

A woman in Moate was going shopping, so she asked her little daughter to go upstairs to the bathroom to check if there was much toothpaste left in the tube. After ten minutes she hadn't returned, so the mother shouted, "Well, is there much left in the tube?"

The little girl shouted back, "Yes, mammy, as much as reaches from the sink to the door."

Two fellows from Tuam won €100 in the lottery so they decided to buy a horse. What they got for their money wasn't exactly a good-looking horse. It looked like two fellows were trying to get out of it.

Sign seen in an undertaker's window in Loughrea:

PAY NOW — GO LATER

A fellow in a bar in Cavan says to the landlord, "Will you give me a free drink if I give you a surefire method of increasing your sales by ten per cent?"

"Sure," says the landlord and proceeds to pour the fellow a pint, which he swallows down in one gulp.

Then he whispers in the landlord's ear, "Fill the glasses up to the top," and heads for the door.

Sign on a restaurant in Navan:

CLOSED FOR LUNCH

A fellow was sitting at a bar in Kells telling the barman the story of his life. "For twenty-five years," he told him, "meself and the wife were blissfully happy."

"Then what happened?" asked the barman.

"Then we met," said yer man.

A farmer from Belmullet went to the doctor and said he was a bit worried about his wife.

"She's only sixty, doctor," he told him, "and yesterday morning she got up as usual at 4.00 a.m., milked the cows, made breakfast for me and the ten kids and the farm worker; then churned the milk, fed the hens and pigs and made dinner for us all; ploughed the lower fields, did the farm accounts before making supper, after which she painted one of the bedrooms and finished off the housework. Around midnight she remarked that she was feeling a bit tired. I'm wondering, doctor, if maybe she needs a tonic or something?"

Two old farmers were having a drink in a bar in Castlebar and were discussing a comet that had recently appeared in the sky.

"What do you think of it?" one asked the other.

The other fellow sipped his pint and said wisely, "They say it's a sure sign of frost."

Notice on a level crossing seen in Clare:

THE AVERAGE TIME IT TAKES A TRAIN TO PASS
THIS LEVEL CROSSING IS TEN SECONDS
– WHETHER YOUR CAR IS ON IT OR NOT

A fellow from Limerick was up in court for motoring offences.

"That's the fifth person you've knocked down with your car this year," said the judge.

"You're wrong there, your honour," said the fellow. "There were only four people but I knocked one of them down twice."

In the good old days, milkmen on the northside of Cork City used to deliver their milk by horse and cart. One milkman was dallying with a local belle and when he came out a street urchin said to him, "Your horse is going nowhere, mister."

"Why is that, son?" he asked.

"Because he's just lost all his petrol."

This fellow in Derry is having some erectile dysfunctional problems so he goes to the doctor.

As he's sitting in the waiting room the female receptionist calls out his name and says loudly, "Are you the man who wants to see the doctor about your impotence?"

Mortified, he retaliates, "No, I want to have a sex-change operation and I just want the name of the doctor who did yours."

Underneath a WET PAINT sign in Kilkenny, someone had scribbled:

THIS IS NOT AN INSTRUCTION

This fellow from Arklow was completely bald so one of his friends suggested that he get a transplant to solve the problem.

"Never," he retorted, "I'd look a right fool with a kidney on my head!"

A girl goes into a restaurant in Derry and orders the turtle soup.

"One turtle soup," the waiter shouts into the kitchen.

"Wait," says the girl, "I've changed my mind, I'll have the pea soup instead."

The waiter shouts out, "Hold that turtle; make it pea."

This fellow from Wexford had a pet duck that he took everywhere with him. One evening he decided to go to the cinema but, knowing that he would not be allowed in if anybody saw his duck, he stuffed it down the front of his trousers, made his way into the cinema and got a seat in the front row.

However, after about half an hour, the duck was gasping for air, so the fellow let him stick his neck out through the flies of his trousers.

There were two girls sitting beside him and one said to the other, "Imelda, that man is exposing himself."

"Look," said Imelda, "when you've seen one, you've seen them all."

"I know," her companion whispered, "But this one is eating my crisps."

Small ad seen in a Mallow newspaper:

HEARSE FOR SALE. NEW ENGINE. ORIGINAL BODY

Notice seen on a shop in Fermoy:

CLOSED UNLESS SOMEBODY WANTS TO
BUY SOMETHING

Two auld wans on top of a bus in Dublin.

"I've just been to Evita," said one of them.

"You didn't get much of a tan," said the other.

Gay Byrne tells the story that he was having a book-signing session in Cork when he heard two of his adoring fans discussing him.

Said one, "Oh, it looks just like him, doesn't it?"

At a funeral mass in Galway the deceased was being praised for his great kindness to animals.

His brother told the congregation that if he ever had to drown a puppy, he always did so in warm water.

A Kerryman up in Dublin for the big match got lost and asked a passing kid, "How do you get to Croke Park?"

The kid replied, "My father usually takes me."

A fellow climbed to the top of Cork's County Hall and threatened to jump unless his demands were met.

"If he doesn't jump soon," a local commentator quipped, "I'm going to miss my bus".

A little lad was travelling with his mother on the top of an open bus in Belfast.

She was heard to say to him, "Take your cap off now, Billy, and let the wind blow the dandruff out of your hair."

Two auld fellas were in a bus passing Ovens Crematorium (I kid you not) in Cork.

One says to the other, "That's where they set the match to my sister. She wanted to be buried in a graveyard, and she doesn't know to this day that she was cremated."

Notice in a Blarney pub:

THE MANAGEMENT WILL NOT BE RESPONSIBLE FOR ANY INJURIES SUSTAINED IN THE MAD RUSH FOR THE DOORS AT CLOSING TIME

At a wedding in Wicklow the best man was proposing toasts to everyone in sight.

Finally, he said, "I would now like to propose a toast to the beautiful bridesmaids."

128

A voice from the back of the room boomed out, "He should have gone to Specsavers."

At another wedding in Meath, the best man's speech started well:

"Marriage is all about honour. Get on 'er, stay on 'er and don't let anybody else on 'er."

A kid in Castlebar was standing on the side of the road bawling crying and a passing woman asked him what the matter was.

"My mother told me not to cross until I saw a zebra crossing, and I waited and waited and waited . . ."

Sign seen on a funeral home in Sligo.

CLOSED FOR LUNCH. IN CASE OF URGENT DEATH RING 123456789

The new Gallery of Modern Art in Dublin was attracting record crowds until a public toilet was opened just round the corner.

A couple of modern parents installed a two-way intercom in their kid's bedroom so they could check on him every half hour.

The first time they used it, they said "Hi Jimmy, are you OK?"

Jimmy replied, "What do you want, wall?"

This little Dublin fellow joined the Japanese air force during World War Two and was assigned to a Kamikaze unit.

The sergeant was briefing them for a mission: "You all fly your planes one mile up into the air. Then you all fly down at a hundled miles an hour. You clash into Amelican ship and kill evelybody. Now, any questions?"

The Dubliner raised his hand and said, "I have a question. Are you out of your tiny mind?"

Headline in the Connacht Tribune:

DEAD GARDA WAS IN THE FORCE
FOR FORTY YEARS

From Claremorris court: "The defendant, who had already been disqualified from driving for life, was disqualified for a further ten years on Thursday last."

Small ad in the Southern Star:

"Miss O'Callaghan wishes to inform the public that she has no male goat this season and refers all clients to the parish priest."

Two fellows in Mullingar were arrested for fighting in a drunken condition and seriously injuring each other. When asked by the judge what they were fighting about they said that they were the best of friends and were fighting about who was the better friend.

Notice on a field near Tullamore:

WALKERS MAY CROSS THIS FIELD FOR FREE
BUT THE BULL CHARGES

A woman from Fair Hill in Cork told a friend that her daughter had just got married and had a "ruptured mass with a paper blessing".